A Note to Parents

DK READERS is a compelling prog
designed in conjunction with leadi
Dr. Linda Gambrell, Professor of E
University. Dr. Gambrell has serve
International Reading Association, National Reading Conference, and College Reading Association.

Beautiful illustrations and superb full-color photographs combine with engaging, easy-to-read stories and informational texts to offer a fresh approach to each subject in the series. Each DK READER is guaranteed to capture a child's interest while developing his or her reading skills, general knowledge, and love of reading.

The five levels of DK READERS are aimed at different reading abilities, enabling you to choose the books that are exactly right for your child:

Pre-level 1: Learning to read

Level 1: Beginning to read

Level 2: Beginning to read alone

Level 3: Reading alone

Level 4: Proficient readers

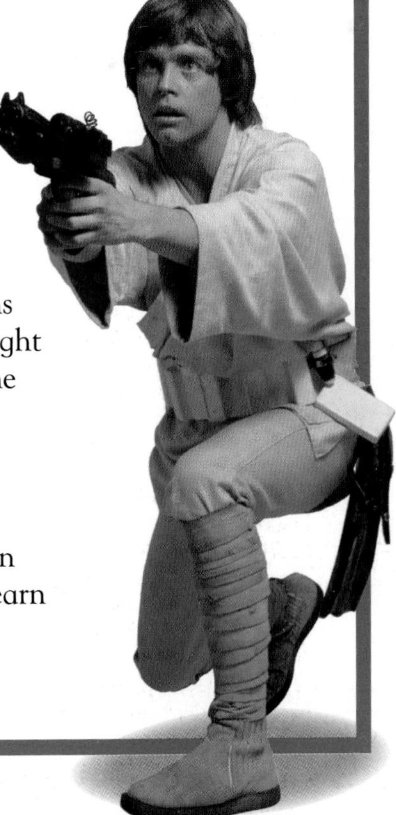

The "normal" age at which a child begins to read can be anywhere from three to eight years old. Adult participation through the lower levels is very helpful for providing encouragement, discussing storylines, and sounding out unfamiliar words.

No matter which level you select, you can be sure that you are helping your child learn to read, then read to learn!

LONDON, NEW YORK,
MELBOURNE, MUNICH, AND DELHI

For Dorling Kindersley
Project Editor Heather Scott
Designer Owen Bennett
Senior Designer Ron Stobbart
Art Director Lisa Lanzarini
Publishing Manager Simon Beecroft
Category Publisher Alex Allan
Production Controller Jen Lockwood
Production Editor Siu Chan

For Lucasfilm
Executive Editor Jonathan W. Rinzler
Art Director Troy Alders
Keeper of the Holocron Leland Chee
Director of Publishing Carol Roeder

Reading Consultant
Linda B. Gambrell, Ph.D.

First published in the United States in 2009
by DK Publishing
375 Hudson Street
New York, New York 10014

12 10 9 8
015-SD410-Dec/2008

Published in Great Britain by Dorling Kindersley Limited.
A catalog record for this book is available from the Library of Congress.

ISBN: 978-0-7566-4518-2 (Paperback)
ISBN: 978-0-7566-4519-9 (Hardback)

Color reproduction by MDP
Printed and bound by L-Rex, China

Discover more at

www.dk.com

www.starwars.com

DK READERS

BEGINNING 1 TO READ

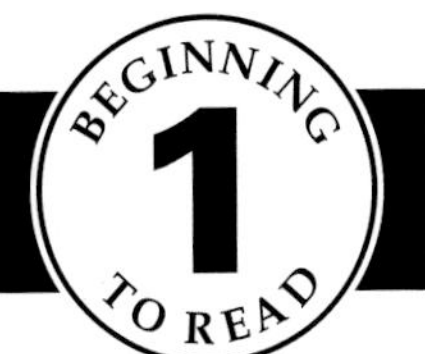

STAR WARS®

LUKE SKYWALKER'S AMAZING STORY

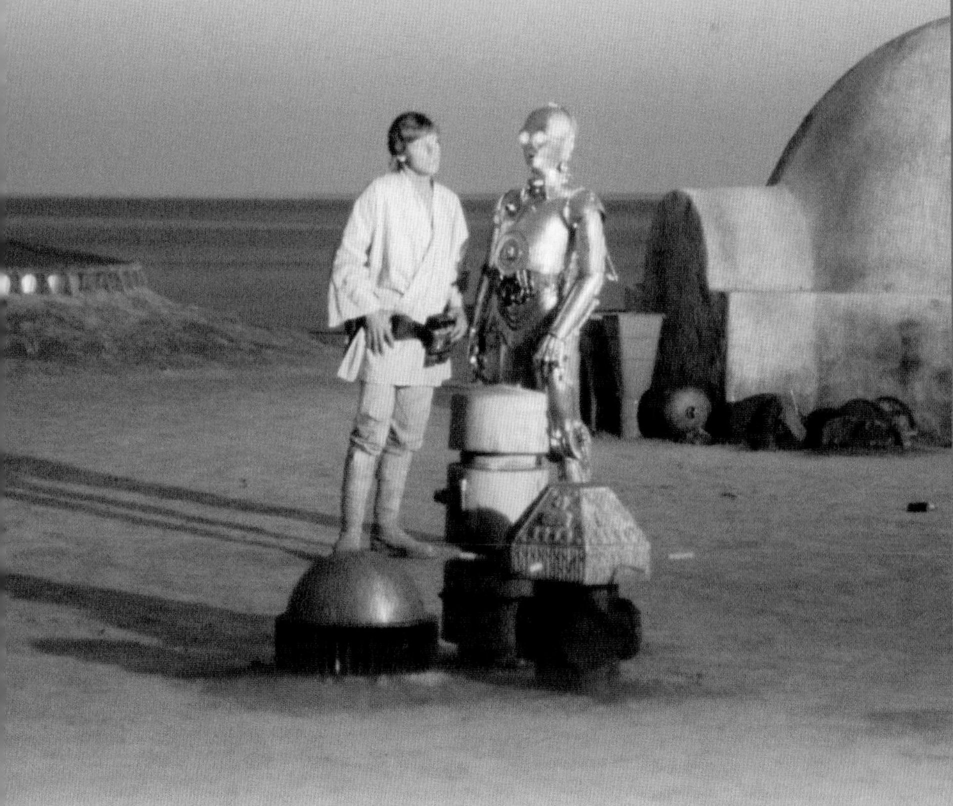

Written by Simon Beecroft

DK

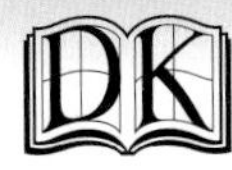

This is Luke.

He dreams of having adventures.

He lives on a far away planet with his aunt and uncle.

His aunt and uncle are called...

Aunt Beru and Uncle Owen.

Uncle Owen is a farmer.

He buys two droids to help him on his farm.

The droids are called...

C-3PO and R2-D2.

R2-D2 has a secret message for a strange old man who lives nearby.

Luke watches the message.

The old man is called...

Obi-Wan Kenobi.

Obi-Wan Kenobi is a Jedi.
He knew Luke's father.

Luke has never met his father.

Luke's father is called...

Anakin Skywalker.

Anakin Skywalker was once a Jedi, like Obi-Wan Kenobi.

But Anakin turned to the dark side of the Force.

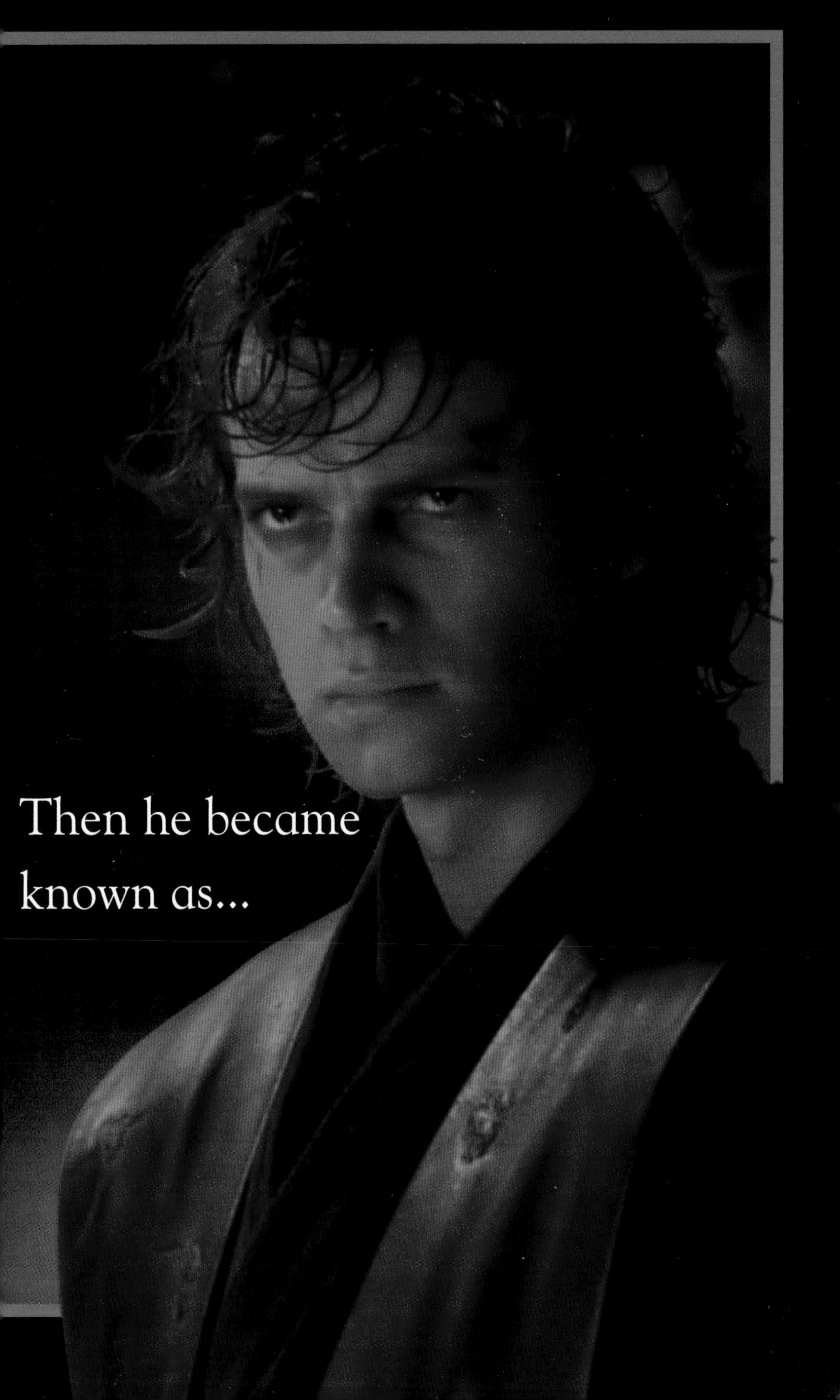

Then he became known as...

Darth Vader.

Darth Vader wants to rule the galaxy.

Some people want to stop him.

They are called Rebels.

Darth Vader has captured the leader of the Rebels.

She is called...

Princess Leia.

Princess Leia put the message inside R2-D2 for Obi-Wan Kenobi. She needs Obi-Wan's help.

Obi-Wan takes Luke to meet two pilots.

The pilots are called...

Han Solo and Chewbacca.

They have a fast spaceship. Obi-Wan asks Han Solo if he will fly them into space.

Han Solo says he will. So...

Chewbacca, Luke, Obi-Wan, Han Solo, C-3PO, and R2-D2 all fly in the fast spaceship to a big space station called the Death Star.

Some soldiers try
to capture them.
The soldiers
are called...

Stormtroopers.

They are Darth Vader's soldiers.
Luke, Han, and Chewbacca fight
the Stormtroopers.

They rescue Princess Leia.
They take Leia to...

The Rebels.

The Rebels attack the Death Star in their spaceships.

Luke blows up the Death Star with a very lucky shot.

Later Luke visits...

Yoda.

Yoda is a Jedi. He lives in a swamp.

Yoda trains Luke to be a Jedi. Luke realizes it is time to meet...

his father, Darth Vader.

Darth Vader wants Luke to
become bad,
like him.

In the end, Luke helps Darth Vader become good again.

Darth Vader turns back into...

Anakin Skywalker, Luke's real father.

Luke takes off Darth Vader's helmet. Luke looks at his father's face.

He is happy to see his father at last.

Quiz!

1. Who is Luke's father?

2. What is this droid's name?

3. Who is this?

4. Who teaches Luke to be a Jedi?

Answers: 1. Anakin Skywalker, 2. C-3PO, 3. Princess Leia, 4. Yoda